ARIZONA

EXPLORE THE UNITED STATES · EXPLORE THE UNITED STATES · EXPLORE THE UNITED STATES · EXPLORE THE UNITED STATES ·

Sarah

Big Buddy BOOKS

VISIT US AT
www.abdopublishing.com

Published by ABDO Publishing Company, PO Box 398166, Minneapolis, MN 55439.

Copyright © 2013 by Abdo Consulting Group, Inc. International copyrights reserved in all countries. No part of this book may be reproduced in any form without written permission from the publisher. Big Buddy Books™ is a trademark and logo of ABDO Publishing Company.

Printed in the United States of America, North Mankato, Minnesota.
022012
092012

PRINTED ON RECYCLED PAPER

Coordinating Series Editor: Rochelle Baltzer
Contributing Editors: BreAnn Rumsch, Marcia Zappa
Graphic Design: Adam Craven
Cover Photograph: *iStockphoto*: ©iStockphoto.com/jose1983.
Interior Photographs/Illustrations: *AP Photo*: Daily News-Sun, Pete Pallagi (p. 27), LM Otero (p. 26), Matt York (p. 25); *Getty Images*: Hulton Archive (p. 23), Frank Zullo/Photo Researchers (p. 30); *iStockphoto*: ©iStockphoto.com/kkant1937 (p. 27), ©iStockphoto.com/legacyimagesphotography (p. 21), ©iStockphoto.com/Nnehring (p. 30), ©iStockphoto.com/photosbyjim (p. 19); *Shutterstock*: Bryan Busovicki (p. 17), EuToch (p. 9), Bill Florence (p. 30), Phillip Lange (p. 30), LouLouPhotos (p. 5), Brett Mulcahy (p. 27), David B. Petersen (p. 13), J. Norman Reid (p. 19), David P. Smith (p. 29), Joao Virissimo (p. 11), Warren Price Photography (p. 26), Andy Z. (p. 9).

All population figures taken from the 2010 US census.

Library of Congress Cataloging-in-Publication Data

Tieck, Sarah, 1976-
  Arizona / Sarah Tieck.
     p. cm. -- (Explore the United States)
  ISBN 978-1-61783-341-0
  1. Arizona--Juvenile literature. I. Title.
  F811.3.T47 2013
  979.1--dc23
                         2012000756

Contents

ONE NATION

The United States is a **diverse** country. It has farmland, cities, coasts, and mountains. Its people come from many different backgrounds. And, its history covers more than 200 years.

Today, the country includes 50 states. Arizona is one of these states. Let's learn more about Arizona and its story!

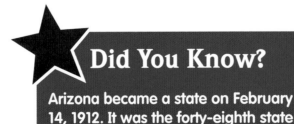

Did You Know?

Arizona became a state on February 14, 1912. It was the forty-eighth state to join the nation.

Arizona is known for its deserts, canyons, and cactus plants.

5

ARIZONA UP CLOSE

Did You Know?

Washington DC is the US capital city. Puerto Rico is a US commonwealth. This means it is governed by its own people.

The United States has four main **regions**. Arizona is in the West.

Arizona has four states on its borders. California and Nevada are west. Utah is north. New Mexico is east. And, the country of Mexico is south.

Arizona has a total area of 113,991 square miles (295,235 sq km). About 6.4 million people live there.

REGIONS OF THE UNITED STATES

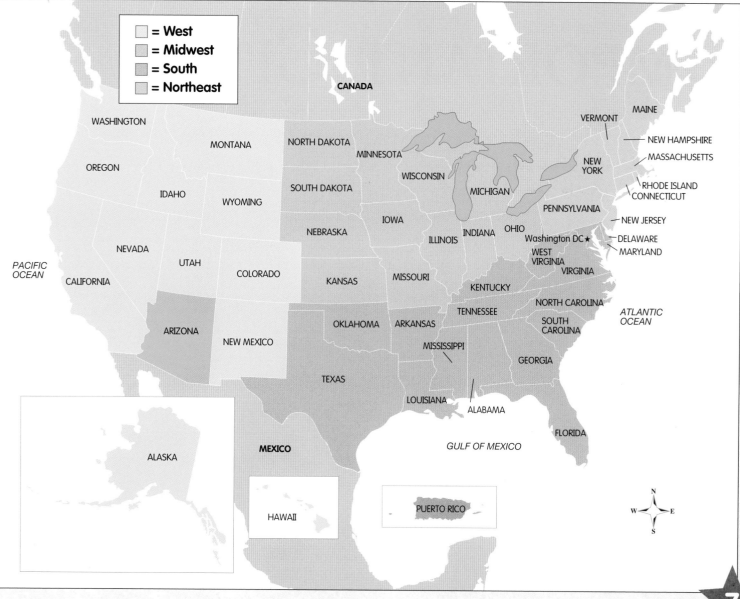

Legend:
- = West
- = Midwest
- = South
- = Northeast

CANADA

WASHINGTON
MONTANA
NORTH DAKOTA
MINNESOTA
VERMONT
MAINE
NEW HAMPSHIRE
OREGON
IDAHO
WYOMING
SOUTH DAKOTA
WISCONSIN
MICHIGAN
NEW YORK
MASSACHUSETTS
RHODE ISLAND
CONNECTICUT
NEVADA
UTAH
COLORADO
NEBRASKA
IOWA
ILLINOIS
INDIANA
OHIO
PENNSYLVANIA
NEW JERSEY
Washington DC ★
DELAWARE
MARYLAND
WEST VIRGINIA
VIRGINIA
PACIFIC OCEAN
CALIFORNIA
KANSAS
MISSOURI
KENTUCKY
NORTH CAROLINA
ATLANTIC OCEAN
ARIZONA
NEW MEXICO
OKLAHOMA
ARKANSAS
TENNESSEE
SOUTH CAROLINA
MISSISSIPPI
GEORGIA
TEXAS
LOUISIANA
ALABAMA
FLORIDA
ALASKA
MEXICO
GULF OF MEXICO
HAWAII
PUERTO RICO

N
W E
S

7

IMPORTANT CITIES

Phoenix (FEE-nihks) is the **capital** of Arizona. It is located in the southern part of the state. And, it is in the Sonoran Desert.

Phoenix is home to 1,445,632 people. It is the largest city in Arizona. It is the sixth-largest city in the country!

Did You Know?

Arizona is one of the fastest-growing states. From 2000 to 2010, its population grew 25 percent!

ARIZONA

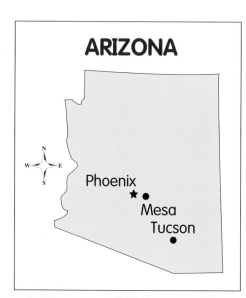

Phoenix ★ ● Mesa
Tucson ●

★★★★★★★★★★★★★★★★★★★★★★★★★★
Today, the capitol building in Phoenix is a museum. The government meets in nearby buildings.

★★★★★★★★★★★★★★★★★★★★★★★★★★
On average, Phoenix has more than 300 sunny days each year!

Arizona's second-largest city is Tucson (TOO-sahn). There are 520,116 people living there. This city is in the Sonoran Desert. It is surrounded by mountains. Many people vacation there because it is warm and sunny all year.

Mesa is Arizona's third-largest city. Its population is 439,041. It is a **suburb** of Phoenix.

The Sonoran Desert has many different plants and animals. One is the saguaro cactus.

Did You Know?

The saguaro (suh-WAHR-uh) cactus is sometimes called "the giant cactus." It can be up to 60 feet (18 m) tall. Some weigh as much as ten tons (9 t)!

ARIZONA IN HISTORY

Arizona's history includes Native Americans, war, and **frontier** life. In the 1500s, the Spanish explored Arizona. Native Americans had lived there for thousands of years.

From 1846 to 1848, the United States and Mexico fought over land. This was called the Mexican-American War. After the war, the United States got part of Arizona. Settlers moved to this new frontier.

★★★★★★★★★★★★★★★★★★★★★★★★★★★★★★★

Native American adobe (uh-DOH-bee) homes can still be seen today in Arizona. Adobe is made from a mix of water, sand, clay, and other natural parts. It dries and hardens in the sun.

13

Timeline

1846

The Mexican-American War began. In 1848, the war ended and Mexico gave part of Arizona to the United States. The United States got the rest of the state in 1853.

1912

Arizona became the forty-eighth state on February 14. It was the last state connected to other states to join the country.

1800s

Mexico won its independence from Spain. Arizona was part of this new country.

1821

Phoenix became Arizona's **capital**.

1889

1930

Scientist Clyde W. Tombaugh discovered Pluto. He was working at the Lowell Observatory in Flagstaff.

2011

The Wallow Fire burned about 800 square miles (2,070 sq km) of land in eastern Arizona. This was the largest wildfire in state history.

1981

Arizona judge Sandra Day O'Connor became the first woman named to the US Supreme Court.

1900s

2000s

The Grand **Canyon** became a national park.

1919

The Hoover Dam was finished. It is on the Colorado River between Arizona and Nevada.

1936

The Saint Louis Cardinals football team became the Arizona Cardinals.

1988

15

ACROSS THE LAND

Arizona has deserts, forests, **canyons**, and **plateaus**. The Grand Canyon is one important part of Arizona's land. The powerful Colorado River formed the canyon. It cut through desert and rock over millions of years!

Many types of animals make their homes in Arizona. Some of these include rattlesnakes, bobcats, coyotes, and jackrabbits.

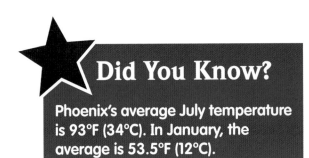

Did You Know?

Phoenix's average July temperature is 93°F (34°C). In January, the average is 53.5°F (12°C).

The Grand Canyon is 277 miles (446 km) long. It goes down about 1 mile (1.6 km) at its deepest point.

EARNING A LIVING

Long ago, people thought Arizona was just a desert. But, the state has **resources** that have created businesses. These businesses offer jobs for people in Arizona.

Arizona's businesses include mining, farming, raising cattle, and building **technology** products. And, many people vacation in the state. So, there are lots of jobs helping visitors.

Cotton (*above*) and citrus fruits (*left*) are some of Arizona's farming products.

Natural Wonder

The Grand **Canyon** is in northern Arizona. In 1919, Grand Canyon National Park was created. It has steep hills, tall rocks, and waterfalls.

About 4 to 5 million people visit the park each year. They bike, hike, camp, and learn about the history and land.

Havasu Falls is near Grand Canyon National Park. Some people swim in the warm, blue-green water!

21

HOMETOWN HEROES

Many famous people have lived in Arizona. Apache (uh-PA-chee) leader Geronimo was born in 1829. No one knows exactly where he was born. Many believe it was near what is now the Arizona-New Mexico border.

During Geronimo's life, Native Americans were mistreated. For many years, Geronimo led fights throughout Arizona to help change life for Native Americans. There was not much change during his life. But, he is still remembered as a strong leader.

Geronimo became known as a powerful fighter.

Sandra Day O'Connor was born in Texas in 1930. But, she grew up near Duncan, Arizona. She became a well-known state senator and judge.

In 1981, President Ronald Reagan named O'Connor to the US Supreme Court. She was the first woman to be given this honor. O'Connor served until 2006.

The Arizona State University law school in Tempe is named for O'Connor.

Tour Book

Do you want to go to Arizona? If you visit the state, here are some places to go and things to do!

★ Taste

Eat food made from cactus (*left*) or try Native American frybread. Arizona is close to Mexico, so Mexican dishes are also popular there.

★ See

Look for southwestern jewelry and art. Native Americans are known for making jewelry from silver, coral, and turquoise.

★ Remember

Visit Native American cliff dwellings. Some are thousands of years old! Scientists say tribes built them into cliffs to stay safe.

★ Cheer

Go to an Arizona Cardinals football game!

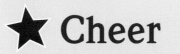

★ Discover

You can't miss the Grand Canyon. Stand on the Skywalk (*left*) for a great view. Or, you could ride mules down into the canyon!

A GREAT STATE

The story of Arizona is important to the United States. The people and places that make up this state offer something special to the country. Together with all the states, Arizona helps make the United States great.

★★★★★★★★★★★★★★★★★★★★★★★★★★★★★★★

The Painted Desert is in northern Arizona.
It was named for its beautiful rock colors.

29

Fast Facts

Date of Statehood:
February 14, 1912

Population (rank):
6,392,017
(16th most-populated state)

Total Area (rank):
113,991 square miles
(6th largest state)

Motto:
"Ditat Deus"
(God Enriches)

Nickname:
Grand Canyon State

State Capital:
Phoenix

Flag:

Flower: Saguaro Cactus Blossom

Postal Abbreviation:
AZ

Tree: Palo Verde

Bird: Cactus Wren

Important Words

canyon a long, narrow valley between two cliffs.

capital a city where government leaders meet.

diverse made up of things that are different from each other.

frontier the edge of settled land, where unsettled land begins.

plateau (pla-TOH) a raised area of flat land.

region a large part of a country that is different from other parts.

resource a supply of something useful or valued.

suburb a town, village, or community just outside a city.

technology (tehk-NAH-luh-jee) the use of science for practical purposes.

Web Sites

To learn more about Arizona, visit ABDO Publishing Company online. Web sites about Arizona are featured on our Book Links page. These links are routinely monitored and updated to provide the most current information available.

www.abdopublishing.com

Index

DISCARD